❧ This book is about ❧

....

A GRANDPARENTS' BOOK
Our Story, Our Life

A Record of Your Life, For Your Family

FLAME TREE
PUBLISHING

Completing This Book

Family histories are an endlessly fascinating subject. The lives of those who have gone before us shape who we are, but we don't always find out all we can. When it comes to our grandparents, we don't always think to ask questions about their lives before they had children and grandchildren, and a whole generation can be forgotten. If you can imagine the interest the early lives of your own grandparents would hold for you, you will realise how important it is to keep a record of your life to hand down to future generations; a record of not just the bare facts, but also your memories and emotions, your achievements and personality. Things that were everyday occurances for you will be fascinating to your grandchildren, and your story will enthral not only them, but one day their children and countless more generations to come.

This book provides a framework for your memories and history, asking questions that you might not have thought of, and providing plenty of space for photographs, momentoes and keepsakes. It has been designed to suit either a single grandparent or a couple, although if the latter you may prefer to each fill in a copy. However you use it, this book will become a treasure trove of family folklore and a rare insight into a personal history. Take the time to recall small details and reminisce, and the result will be a rich tapestry of enthralling family history to give to your grandchildren. Whatever the story of your life, you will be able to record it here and help to give your descendents a true flavour of who you were and the times you have lived through, something no school text book can convey quite as well.

Contents

THE CHILDHOOD YEARS

The Beginning...... 6
Brothers & Sisters...... 8
Home Life...... 10
Social Life...... 14
Schooldays...... 16

FAMILY HISTORY

Your Parents...... 22
Your Grandparents...... 24

ADULT YEARS

Working Life...... 28
When You Met...... 30
Your Wedding...... 32
Married Life...... 34

IN YOUR LIFETIME

Friends & Homes...... 38
Holidays...... 40
In Your Lifetime...... 42

THE NEXT GENERATION

The Next Generation...... 46

THE CHILDHOOD YEARS

The Beginning
Brothers & Sisters
Home Life
Social Life
Schooldays

The Beginning

What is your full name?

....

Were these names chosen for a reason?

....

....

When and where were you born?

....

How much did you weigh at birth?

....

PLACE YOUR PHOTO HERE

PLACE YOUR PHOTO HERE

How old were your parents when you were born?

Brothers & Sisters

How many brothers and sisters did you have? ....

NAME	DATE BORN	PLACE BORN
....	....	....
....	....	....
....	....	....
....	....	....

Who was the best behaved?

....

Who was the naughtiest?

....

Who did you fight with?

....

Who did you get on well with?

....

PLACE YOUR PHOTO HERE

What do you particularly remember about your brothers and sisters
from your childhood?

....

....

....

....

PLACE YOUR PHOTO HERE

What were their occupations as adults?

....

....

....

What are your memories of them in adult life?

....

....

....

Home Life

Where did you live when you were young?

....

Did you have a bedroom of your own? ....

What do you remember about your home?

....

....

....

....

Did you have a garden? ....

Did you move when you were young? ....

Where else did you live?

PLACE

....

....

....

....

DATE

....

....

....

....

What are your earliest memories?

....

....

....

....

What was your favourite toy?

....

....

What games did you play?

....

....

PLACE YOUR PHOTO HERE

Home Life

Did you have any pets?

....

What were your favourite and least favourite meals?

FAVOURITE

....

....

....

LEAST FAVOURITE

....

....

....

Did you ever argue with your parents?

....

....

Were you given pocket money? ....

If so, how much was it?   Did you have to earn it?

....

....

....

What did you like to spend it on?

....

....

Did you do any chores around the house in order to earn your pocket money?

....

....

Which was your best birthday and why was it so special?

....

....

What was the best present you ever received? ....

Did you have any family traditions at Christmas?

....

....

Social Life

Were you allowed to listen to music? ....

What sort of music did you like?

....

....

PLACE YOUR PHOTO HERE

Were you allowed to wear what you wanted?

....

Can you remember the first clothes you bought with your own money?

....

....

Did you have a favourite actor or actress?

....

....

Was there anywhere you used to go to regularly in the evenings or at weekends?

....

....

Who was your first kiss with?   How old were you?

....

Who was your first boyfriend or girlfriend?   How long were you together?

....

Schooldays

Describe your first school. How old were you when you went there?

What do you remember about your teachers? Did you like it there?

....

....

....

Which school did you move on to after that?

....

How did you get to school? ....

Did you have a best friend? ....

Who were your other friends?

NAMES

....

....

....

....

....

What were your favourite and least favourite subjects?

FAVOURITE

LEAST FAVOURITE

....

....

....

....

Who was your favourite teacher and why?

....

....

How much homework were you given? ....

Did you have to wear a uniform? Describe it.

....

....

PLACE YOUR PHOTO HERE

Schooldays

Were you well-behaved or did you ever get into trouble at school?

....

Did you learn any musical instruments? ....

Were you good at sports?   What did you play?

....

Did you have a part-time or Saturday job when you were older?

....

How old were you when you left school? ....

PLACE YOUR PHOTO HERE

18

Did you go on to further studies? ....

If so, where did you go and what did you study?

....

If not, what did you do?

....

What qualifications did you gain?

SUBJECT   QUALIFICATION

....

....

....

What are your best memories of this time?

....

....

....

....

....

....

....

FAMILY
HISTORY

Your Parents
Your Grandparents

Your Parents

What was your father's name? ....

When and where was he born?

DATE BORN

PLACE BORN

....

PLACE YOUR PHOTO HERE

What was his occupation? ....

What were his interests and hobbies?

....

....

What was your mother's full name before she was married? ....

When and where was she born?

DATE BORN

PLACE BORN

....

Describe her appearance. What were her interests and hobbies?

....

....

Did she have a job? Did she continue to work after her marriage?

....

What are your fondest memories of her?

....

....

PLACE YOUR PHOTO HERE

Your Grandparents

What were your father's parents' names?

NAME   DATE BORN   PLACE BORN

....

....

What were their occupations?

GRANDFATHER   GRANDMOTHER

....

When did they die? How old were they?

GRANDFATHER   GRANDMOTHER

....

PLACE YOUR PHOTO HERE   PLACE YOUR PHOTO HERE

What were your mother's parents' names?

NAME   DATE BORN   PLACE BORN

....

....

What were their occupations?

GRANDFATHER   GRANDMOTHER

....

When did they die? How old were they?

GRANDFATHER   GRANDMOTHER

....

PLACE YOUR PHOTO HERE

ADULT YEARS

Working Life
When You Met
Your Wedding
Married Life

Working Life

What was your first full-time job? ....

Did you enjoy it?

....

....

How much were you paid? ....

Was it easy or hard to make ends meet?

....

....

How did you travel to work?   What hours did you work?

....

What were your colleagues like?

....

....

How long did you stay in your first job?

....

Where have you worked since?

....

....

Where did you most enjoy working?

....

....

What was your main occupation during your working life? ....

What did you want to be when you were a child?

....

When You Met

How did you first meet your future husband or wife?

....

....

....

How old were you both? ....

What were your first impressions of each other?

....

....

Where did you go on your first date?

....

....

....

....

....

....

....

How long were you together before you got engaged? ....

How long was your engagement? ....

How did the proposal take place?

....

....

....

....

Describe the engagement ring.

....

....

PLACE YOUR PHOTO HERE

PLACE YOUR PHOTO HERE

Your Wedding

What was the date of your wedding? ....

How old were you both when you got married?

....

Where did the ceremony take place? ....

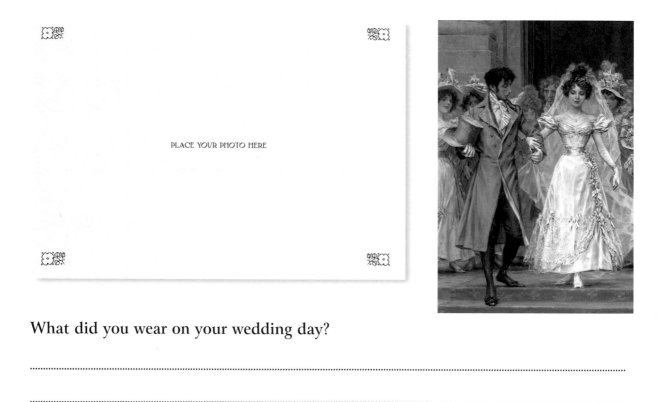

PLACE YOUR PHOTO HERE

What did you wear on your wedding day?

....

....

Who was the best man?   Did you have any bridesmaids?

....

How many guests came? ....

Did you have a reception? ....

Where was it held?

....

....

....

....

What did you eat?

....

....

....

....

Did you dance to a special song?

....

What are your main memories of your wedding day?

....

....

Did you have a honeymoon?

....

....

....

....

....

....

PLACE YOUR PHOTO HERE

Married Life

Where was your first home together? Describe it.

....

....

....

Why did you choose to live there?

....

....

How long did you live there? ....

How long did you wait before having children? ....

PLACE YOUR PHOTO HERE

How many children did you have? ....

NAME	DATE BORN	BIRTH WEIGHT
....	....	....
....	....	....
....	....	....
....	....	....

What are your favourite memories from when they were small?

....

....

Was there anywhere you went to often on family holidays?

....

....

PLACE YOUR PHOTO HERE

IN
YOUR
LIFETIME

Friends & Homes
Holidays
In Your Lifetime

Friends & Homes

Who have been your best friends during your life?

....

How did you meet them and get to know them?

....

Why do you think you get on so well?

....

....

What are the happiest memories you have of your friends?

....

PLACE YOUR PHOTO HERE

PLACE YOUR PHOTO HERE

Can you remember all the places you have lived during your lifetime?

ADDRESS	DATE	WHO LIVED THERE WITH YOU
....	....	....
....	....	....
....	....	....
....	....	....
....	....	....
....	....	....
....	....	....

Which was your favourite place to live and why?

....

....

....

PLACE YOUR PHOTO HERE

Holidays

What sort of holidays did you go on as a child?

....

Where was your favourite place to visit as a child and why?

....

....

PLACE YOUR PHOTO HERE

Have you been back to any of these places with your own children? Was it as good as you remembered?

....

....

Did you go on any memorable holidays after you left school?

....

....

Have you ever lived in another country? Did you enjoy it?

....

....

PLACE YOUR PHOTO HERE

What has been your favourite place to visit as an adult and why?

....

....

Where would you like to visit that you haven't yet been to?

....

In Your Lifetime

Have you ever met any famous people? What were the circumstances?

....

....

....

Have you witnessed any exciting or significant historical events?

....

....

What have been the most important historical events to take place in your lifetime?

....

....

PLACE YOUR PHOTO HERE

Do you have any regrets?

....

....

What are you most proud of?

....

....

What is the best piece of advice you ever received?

....

....

....

Which person in your life has had the best influence on you?

....

....

....

If you could choose any occupation for a single day, what would it be and why?

....

....

....

THE NEXT GENERATION

The Next Generation

The Next Generation

How many grandchildren do you currently have? ....

NAME	AGE	DATE OF BIRTH
....	....	....
....	....	....
....	....	....
....	....	....
....	....	....
....	....	....

What was the grandchild you are writing this for like as a baby?

....

....

PLACE YOUR PHOTO HERE

PLACE YOUR PHOTO HERE

If you could give them one piece of advice, what would it be?

....

....

....

Publisher and Creative Director: Nick Wells
Project Editor: Sarah Goulding
Designer: Lucy Robins
Picture Research: Frances Bodiam

FLAME TREE PUBLISHING
Crabtree Hall, Crabtree Lane
Fulham, London SW6 6TY
United Kingdom

www.flametreepublishing.com

First published in 2005

11 13 12

15 17 19 20 18 16

Picture Credits

Front cover and Page 1: *Maternity*, by Paul Leroy (1860–1908), © Christie's Images Ltd
Page 2 (t to b): *Der Blumenzuchter (The Gardener)*, by Herman Kern (1839–1912), © Christie's Images Ltd;
Alleluya, by Thomas Cooper Gotch (1854–1931), © Christie's Images Ltd
Pages 4–5,17 and 19: *Le Retour de l'Ecole (Back to School)*, by Henry Jules Jean Geoffroy (1853–1924), © Christie's Images Ltd
Page 7: *Motherly Love*, by Ferenc Innocent (b. 1859), © Christie's Images Ltd
Page 8: *An Impromptu Ball* 1899, by Eva Roos, © Christie's Images Ltd
Page 9: *On The Beach*, by Edward Henry Potthast (1857–1927), © Christie's Images Ltd
Page 11: *Young Girl in a New York Garden*, by John George Brown (1831–1913), © Christie's Images Ltd
Page 12: *Three Little Kittens*, by Joseph Clark (1834–1926), © Christie's Images Ltd
Page 13: *Gathering the Grapes*, by George Smith (1829–1901), © Christie's Images Ltd
Page 14: *La Tarantella*, by Leon Perrault (1832–1908), © Christie's Images Ltd
Page 15: *The Flower Garland*, by Charles Edouard De Beaumont (1812–88), © Christie's Images Ltd
Pages 16 and 36–37: *Deux Fillettes*, by Pierre Auguste Renoir (1841–1919), © Christie's Images Ltd
Page 18: *After Class*, by Marc Louis Benjamin Vautier (1829–98), © Christie's Images Ltd
Pages 20–21: *Some Good Advice*, by Hendrik Jacobus Scholten (1824–1907), © Christie's Images Ltd
Page 22: *Watching Father Work*, by Albert Neuhuijs (1844–1914), © Christie's Images Ltd
Page 23: *Mother's Day*, by William Feron (1858–94), © Christie's Images Ltd
Page 25: *A Sunday Afternoon*, by Thomsen Carl, © Christie's Images Ltd
Pages 26–27: *Preparing the Table*, by Michael Peter Ancher (1849–1927), © Christie's Images Ltd
Page 29: *Die Kleinen Gartnerinnen*, by Edmund Louyot (fl. 1888–1909), © Christie's Images Ltd
Page 30: *My Lady is a Widow and Childless*, by Marcus Stone RA (1840–1921), © Christie's Images Ltd
Pages 32–33: *After the Wedding*, by Frederik Hendrik, © Christie's Images Ltd
Page 34: *Mother, Sara, and the Baby*, by Mary Cassatt (1845–1926), © Christie's Images Ltd
Page 35: *On the Sands*, by Julius Ehrentraut (1841–1923), © Christie's Images Ltd
Page 39: *The Cottage Garden*, by Alfred Augustus Glendening (1861–1907), © Christie's Images Ltd
Page 40: *Picking May Blossom*, by William Kay Blacklock (b. 1872), © Christie's Images Ltd
Page 41: *At the Waters Edge*, by Charles Wilda (1854–1907), © Christie's Images Ltd
Page 42: *Picking Daisies*, by Hermann Seeger (1857–1920), © Christie's Images Ltd
Pages 44–45 and back cover: *Kaffeepause*, by Alexander Max Koester (1864–1932), © Christie's Images Ltd
Page 47: *The Children of Sir H. Hussey Vivian*, by George Elgar Hicks RA (1824–1914), © Christie's Images Ltd

A CIP record for this book is available from the British Library.

ISBN 978 1 84451 323 9

Printed in China

This book was completed on